# The Mindset Mission

## *Techniques To Create A Positive Mindset*

## *To Achieve Your Potential*

Danielle Simpson

The Mindset Mission:
Techniques To Create A Positive Mindset To Achieve Your
Potential

The book information is catalogued as follows;
Author Name(s): Danielle Simpson
Title: The Mindset Mission: Techniques To Create A Positive
Mindset To Achieve Your Potential

Description; First Edition
1st Edition, 2021
Book Design & Typesetting by Michael Maloney

ISBN: 978-1-914447-00-6 (paperback)

ISBN: 978-1-914447-01-3 (ebook)

Published by That Guy's House
www.ThatGuysHouse.com

To G

Thank you
lots of love
Dani
x

*This quote has changed my perception of life
and I really want to share this with you*

## 'Trust the Process'

# Contents

# Note from the Author: #sorrynotsorry

## Hello and welcome!

Thank you so much for grabbing a copy of my book. I am so grateful and excited for you to read my story, but more importantly, for you to take away the teachings and implement them into your own lives. So, you're probably thinking what is this book all about? Well, it's highlighting the need to conquer your unkind mind. The unkind mind to me is the inner critic, that little negative voice that is always the first to jump in.

I went through a very challenging time in my life, which made me question the point of continuing my shitty little life. I know there are many people out there who have suffered worse events and others who just don't feel like they belong or know what they are meant to do here on earth. I felt exactly the same and I consider myself a strong-minded woman but sometimes the world feels against you and you just want to throw the towel in.

The positive is...

I didn't throw in the towel; I found a set of tools and techniques to re-wire my brain and stop beating myself up. I have always been my hardest critic and don't get me wrong, I'm nowhere near 'perfect' but I do care and treat myself with more respect now.

Side note - there is no such thing as perfect!

In this book, you will learn and, hopefully embrace the techniques, which will create positive changes in your mind and life. The goal for this book is to recognise the negative thought patterns, shift your mindset for the positive, open up incredible opportunities that allow you to appreciate and love yourself as well as others. I would love this book to help everyone want to get out of bed in the mornings and look forward to the day ahead. In this day and age life can be too much at times and misfortune can surprise you. I don't believe we are taught how to deal with it, especially not in school, and as an adult, there isn't much support at all.

Upsetting truth...

In the UK Suicide rates are increasing and when you call for help you are put on a very long waiting list with no check-up calls, which is really no help at all. Don't get me wrong, I'm not putting down the professionals; the work they do is incredible, however the system is stretched, and a lot of people are not getting the support they need and some people are too embarrassed to ask for help. I was embarrassed in the beginning as thought I would look weak.

So, I am writing this book with hope it connects with you and so you can take some golden nuggets away to use moving forward. Giving you the want and will to spring out of bed in the morning with a smile on your face, looking forward to the day ahead. Life is meant to be fun; I like to look at it as a game. You will be tested along the way, how you respond will determine the outcome. Let's level up together!

I must state I am not a doctor or a therapist or a scientist for that matter. I am a qualified mindset and meditation coach who has experienced some shit along the way. I asked the universe for help at a VERY dark time in my life and found some incredible people and ways that have most definitely got me into a lighter, happier and healthier place.

I also must share, before you continue, that some parts of the book get dark, VERY dark. If depression, death, divorce and suicidal thoughts upset you, if you don't like to swear or hear the situation for exactly what it is, then maybe this book isn't for you. I have been completely honest throughout the pages, as I believe you have to be authentic and not ashamed of your vulnerability, to change for the better. So, grab a cup of tea and let's get stuck in.

I hope you enjoy this book and learn how to dim the unkind mind and switch that shitty situation.

 x

# Part One

# My Self-limiting beliefs throughout childhood.
# #AlltheBullshit

Let's start at the start. Childhood. This is where most limiting beliefs are created in the early stages of your life. Up to the age of 12 you would have encountered a number of experiences that would have programmed a self-belief. These are the stories you tell yourself; they can be positive or negative, mainly negative unfortunately. Statistics from the National Science Foundation show that our thoughts in our mind are, on average, 80% negative and we have between 12,000 to 60,000 per day. 95% are repetitive thoughts, which means we are walking around day in day out beating ourselves up with the same horrid thoughts. Awesome hey? My aim for this book is to help, inspire and train you to reduce that percentage.

So let's get into my self-limiting beliefs and where they were created. I'm sharing to see if you can relate and also understand how life experiences can create such thoughts.

At the age of eight my parents divorced. Which really crushed me as I was a proper little daddy's girl. I absolutely loved when he would come home from work and I followed him around the house, would sunbathe with him, put make up on him, I was his shadow. So, when my parents separated, and he moved out, it really affected me. I found out my parents were divorcing by overhearing a phone call my dad was having with his friend. I was crushed, crying in my bed. I felt like I couldn't talk to my dad as I wasn't meant to be listening as I should have been asleep. Feeling confused, alone and so upset, I lay in bed all night crying. During the next few days anger kicked in, as I didn't understand why my mum suddenly hated him and wanted him gone. I physically stopped talking to her as couldn't believe she had done this. Now I look back at what was a terribly hard time for my mum, going through a marriage break up and her daughter giving her the cold shoulder because of it. Only a week passed, and my mum cracked, she told me why dad had to go. He had been unfaithful and broken my mum's trust resulting in the family breaking, including my little heart.

This was my first experience that love fades and trust can be broken. Seeing my mum struggle emotionally, beating herself up daily, really imprinted on me, and the limiting beliefs; 'you're not good enough' was sparked in my mind.

My parents, both relatively young, acted very differently. Dad was out loving his new single life, and mum, feeling trapped with us kids, became angry and resentful.

Dad quickly met my step mum, which made matters so much worse. Let me paint the picture for you, she wasn't at all an evil step mum like poor Cinderella had however, she was a young, jealous Leo who loved to party. She didn't have children of her own, which caused problems, as she couldn't understand why my parents had to remain so close and in contact. She was a fiery character, and if she had something to say she wouldn't hold back. This often resulted in arguments between her and my mum, which was sometimes scary for a young child. It became known to everyone that they hated each other, which then created the self-limiting belief that my step mum hated me, as everyone told me I was so much like my mum. I had my mum's dark thick hair and big brown eyes and sassy ways, making me incredibly cautious of my step mum growing up.

When my brother and I would stay over at dad's we would have fun with him, and if my step mum was there, eventually I would relax and have fun with her too. Dad would always treat us; he was always so generous. He would let us stay up late and eat what we wanted. However, as a kid, it was such a horrible and uncomfortable situation to be in. I enjoyed my time with dad, which I loved, but then would feel guilty for mum as I knew she was at home unhappy and overthinking; What did I do wrong? As an adult I have also experienced this, and it's the most painful feeling ever, I'll go into more detail later in Part 1.

When I would come home mum would ask, "How was the weekend?"

I would play it down for fear of hurting her more. So, at age eight or nine I had become the world's best people pleaser. In my mind if I said it was alright then mum wouldn't get upset or jealous. 'Don't speak your truth' became my new limiting belief. I have continued this belief throughout adulthood, always wanting to make sure the other person feels good and suppressing my feelings and or wants.

As time went on my dad and step mum became more serious, but the relationship between them and my mum was still poisonous, unfortunately. Dad had always been a hard worker, however, his priorities started shifting from us on to work more and more, and of course to my step mum. He would not pick us up from school like he promised, and he missed our sports day and other activities. All these events added up and started to make me feel resentful and unloved, like he didn't want to spend time with us anymore. I would get so upset, just wanting attention from dad. This was more evidence for my self-limiting beliefs 'You are not good enough' which grew into 'You're unlovable'.

As we go through life our minds collect evidence to prove the point we are telling ourselves and sometimes, if the evidence doesn't prove your story, the mind doesn't bring awareness to the said evidence. For example, my dad always tells me he loves me, however, in my mind he doesn't because of the all the evidence I have been collecting over the years and I created that story in my head.

In 2019, 42% of marriages ended in divorce but this statistic has actually decreased over the years. However, when my parents got a divorce the rate was a lot higher. I'm not sure if you can relate to being a kid who went through divorce but I'm sure you know a kid who has experienced it, that could be a friend, a cousin, and/or a grandchild. Whoever, we can still all agree Divorce is hard for the kids. It's a time in their little lives that never fully makes sense, huge changes that they didn't see coming or know how to handle. Most kids project on themselves; it's my fault. Maybe if I ate all my dinner, daddy wouldn't get mad then mummy wouldn't have kicked him out. There is no right or wrong for the parents, all I'm sharing is divorce is hard and adding new family members is even harder.

# Evidence collected over the Years #storytime

As I grew up my relationship with my dad dwindled over the years, which just added to the self-limiting beliefs. At age eleven my mum moved my brother and I to Australia to start a better life, which it was an incredible experience. We were always at the beach and I remember being a kid again, not having to worry much about anything, always smiling and laughing with my friends.

During that time, my step mum had my little sister, which my mind told me we were out of sight and out of mind. Obviously, the distance, the time difference and now a baby sister created a thicker wedge between dad and me. Mum always told me dad loved me deeply, and just because he has had another baby girl doesn't change that but like I said before my mind wouldn't listen, as that's not the evidence I was collecting. Dad doesn't love me was the main headline in my mind and now he has replaced me. When you're a child you don't understand information the same as when you're an adult, there is no logic. So, my dad couldn't love us equally in my head. For starters: I didn't live ANYWHERE near him, and secondly, I was from his first marriage, which he didn't want anymore.

After two years my mum moved us to Canada slightly closer to home but still miles and miles away. I was a teenager at this point and just got my first proper boyfriend, I was absolutely smitten. I would shower him with gifts, skip school to spend time with him, drink alcohol, do drugs, whatever he wanted to do, I did. I had no boundaries in place at all, just loved the male attention I was getting. He cheated on me. I took him back which was a counter reaction to my mum's decision years ago. I had witnessed how upset she had been and how it still was affecting her from making that one decision. I decided to 'forgive' him.

Side- note: This never works, once the relationship has lost trust it is broken, that's the relationship done in my new eyes. There is a song out at the moment called: 'Know your worth' by Khalid and Disclosure which is all about knowing your worth and finding someone who also knows your worth! SOOOO relevant and a great tune, download now!

This relationship lasted another four years, eight years in total. We both moved back to the UK and went to university together. Unfortunately, once graduated he decided I wasn't the girl for him and moved back to Canada and if we fast forward to present day, he has now married the girl he cheated on me with. As Shaunagh Philips would say "CONGRATS HUN!"

During these years, my dad and step mum had got engaged, which I found out over Facebook! Got to love social media keeping families connected. More evidence I wasn't even a second thought in my dad's mind, he didn't even tell me he was thinking of proposing. However, depression had swamped my step mum due to her mother passing at a young age. My step mum then turned to alcohol to numb her pain, which was the start of the dark years to come.

After graduating university, freshly dumped by whom I thought was the love of my life, I was now homeless too. During university my mum had moved into a smaller home so there was unfortunately no room in the inn. I had to approach my dad about moving into his house, surprisingly he and my step mum agreed.

I was shocked they said yes as my step mum had recently had my second sister, she was a little miracle baby, 10 weeks premature but so strong. At first it was working well, I was rarely there working full time at a local gym but then Halloween hit, which was 28 days after me moving in. My step mum was drunk and clearly annoyed at me for something, that's another thing about my family no one knows how to communicate sober and respectfully. We all get blind drunk and then scream how we really feel, which, as you can imagine, works incredibly well however, it stems back to my self- limiting belief 'Don't speak your truth'.

On this particular night it ended up me storming out so upset and staying at my grandparents. The next day I got a text from my dad agreeing with my step mum that I shouldn't return. This absolutely devastated me. He had literally chosen her over me, confirming the limiting beliefs 'You're not good enough and unloved'. He told me, 'he doesn't need the Agg' (Aggravation) so it's probably best for me to move into my grandparents.

(Quick back-story: Both my grandparents were early 80s and my grandad was dying of cancer at the time. Rest in Peace Grandad, love you lots!)

9

As you can imagine that was the perfect place to live for a young girl in her early twenties, dealing with so much recent rejection. #positivevibes

My grandad was my world; he looked after me from 6 weeks old up until he passed away. He was a consistent male who showed me love always so when he left, I left. I did what I do best, RUN! I went back to Australia for 8 weeks to drink myself numb and forget my shitty little life.

When I returned home, I remained distanced from my dad. Still living with my Nan and still working hard at a local gym I was trying to work my way up to management. A couple years had passed, one terribly controlling relationship later, which I had failed to set boundaries again and I was now living back with my mum as my younger brother had moved out with his girlfriend at the time and once again I had nowhere to go after leaving the ex. I moved out of our apartment that we had together, leaving him everything including a sofa my dad had given us. (Evidence dad does care and loves me, however my mind decided to ignore that)

I was happy to be living with my mum again and I had success-fully got my management role in the gym, I was focused on that and getting myself back on my feet after the breakup.

## #WhenShitHitTheFan

It was a year later; 2018, October to be exact. I wasn't happy, I was all over the place, my mindset was negative, and I felt physically exhausted all the time but couldn't relax or focus on anything. Anyone felt like this before?

I had moved to Manchester, working what I thought was going to be my dream job, renovating a gym. However, I was so miserable and hated it. Plus to top it off I was sleeping with a married man - what a hypocrite! I KNOW! My childhood had been ruined by this exact act and here I was doing the same. I hated myself but couldn't stop. I told myself we loved each other; we were childhood sweethearts who's timing was off. He always told me, I was the one, but he was trapped at the minute, and like an idiot I fully believed him. I would tell myself we were soul mates and he had just made a mistake marrying her.

The phrase daddy issue has probably sprung to your mind. That phrase pisses me off! Women may have 'daddy issues' however they have been neglected from love and care growing up so when they are presented with some form of attention from a male they go weak at the knees, even when they know they most definitely shouldn't!! Plus, remember I thought I was unlovable, so there is no way I would attract a guy who is actually wanting and willing to love me fully. Will explain what I mean by attract in Part 2 of the book.

So, on that day when I got the life changing call from my dad, my gut said YES! My dad and I still didn't have a great relationship at this point, we had drifted apart massively but I was desperate to improve the relationship and I knew that saying yes that would help. He had never asked for help before, so I knew it was serious plus I was in a shit place and saw this as a great way to run from my failures. It couldn't get any worst right?

WRONG!

My dad needed help with my little sisters while my step mum got help with her alcohol problem. Unfortunately, she was in a deep depression now. When she had previously been to the doctors for help they wouldn't help as said she had to deal with the depression before they tackle the alcohol, but she dealt with all her pain and suffering by numbing it through alcohol. Which yes, it temporarily worked but doesn't solve the problem. Many Brits turn to alcohol during a problem and I am no saint, I've definitely drowned myself in wine trying to numb my feelings many times.

Social services were involved with the situation, as the drinking had gotten so bad. They were monitoring to see who was providing a duty of care for my sisters. They didn't want my step mum to live with them or look after them. However, my dad worked away a lot and obviously couldn't stop working, he had bills to pay and mouths to feed.

I knew it was important to step in and help, however, I was struggling with the role. Never had I looked after children before plus my relationship with my sisters wasn't fantastic. I barely saw them, as I would try to avoid the household. I always felt uncomfortable around my step mum since the Halloween argument and when she drank she was so unpredictable.

For this to work my focus had to be the girls and not let my previous absence affect that. To be honest that wasn't the only thing I was struggling with, leaving my job which I hated but I had worked hard, been recognised for that and had a few promotions under my belt. It wasn't just a job it was my identity, my career that was now gone. Deep down I knew if anything had happened to my sisters I couldn't have lived with myself if I had stayed in Manchester, so I definitely had made the right decision, but I was struggling to accept and adjust. I felt like I had taken a huge step back moving in with dad again and now had no career. A new self-limiting belief was created; I'm nothing and have nothing to show for myself, which I would tell others and myself daily.

A few months past and emotions were still very high as my step mum wasn't getting any better and was randomly showing up causing havoc. Both my sisters' anxiety and mine was through the roof, on edge always waiting to see what was going to happen next.

Then one morning the doorbell rang, it was police, they had come to arrest my dad! My step mum had accused him of rape.

I was petrified and so confused in floods of tears. I had no idea what to do and knew dad would never do that. Absolutely devastated and so scared. My little sisters were in their bedroom watching a movie. I heard the girls' confusion; they had heard the commotion downstairs and jumped up to look out the window; watching dad walk up the driveway. I ran into comfort them, not knowing what to say and feeling like a failure in this moment not being able to protect them. I lied and said "oh nothing to worry about he is just helping the police with some important work."

I knew the girls didn't believe me but what was I meant to say? Still sobbing I called my brother for guidance and for dad's boss' phone number as he was meant to be flying to Scotland for work later that afternoon. Luckily, my brother and I have a great relationship, this news knocked him for six too but, being the supportive guy he is, he left work immediately to be there for the girls and I.

Later that night around 2am, dad arrived home. Once realising whom it was, I ran downstairs and gave my dad a huge hug. Overwhelmed but glad he was home, we sat in the front room discussing all the dramas of the day. Dad was released due to a text my step mum sent the night in question. She had pleaded for dad to stay the night, as she hated being alone, the police knew it was a false allegation and advised dad to get an injunction out on her.

For me that was the final straw for my step mum. I was really struggling with the allegation as that could have ended very badly, not just for my dad but for all of us. I was so anxious and stuck in fight mode. Struggling to sleep I became very ratty and snappy, super emotional, and bursting into tears at the most random things. However, dad had seemed to have brushed off the whole situation and had put it down to my step mum being dramatic. I did not feel the same way and was finding it so hard to deal with, let alone dad being so cool about the whole thing. I couldn't understand him, which made me angrier.

Dad finally agreed with the police and social services to file for the injunction. He then sorted out my step mum a flat close by. She moved in at the end of November, She had her own little space to make it safe and show social services she was a good mum just in a rough patch. I thought this was the start of her road to recovery and my anxiety started to calm slightly.

Sadly, the injunction and flat had made her feel incredibly lonely, which led her to drink more. She was always a very angry drunk and always the victim, which doesn't sit well with social services, they want to see that you understand you have a problem and want to change for the sake of the children. They classed dad as the enabler as he gave her money for food and life amenities, which left him in a difficult position.

One glimmer of hope and light at the end of the tunnel was that she had previously been arrested for drink driving, resulting in a driving ban and compulsory AA help. This was the break my step mum needed and if she didn't stick to it, it would result in jail time, which we all knew she didn't want. She began attending but then shortly after, due to sickness, stopped.

In late January 2019 she passed away from liver failure.

2019 was 21 days old and I got the call. My step mum wasn't going to make it. These words paralysed me, my first thought was I had to pick up my gorgeous baby sisters from school, knowing their mum was in hospital about to pass away. I broke down that afternoon as the thought of their little faces and hearts breaking into tiny little pieces hearing this horrendous news. I cried and cried but as I approached the school knew I had to be strong for them. I gave them both a huge cuddle at the school gate and was determined to have a lovely afternoon together; we watched our favourite movie and drank hot chocolate waiting for dad to return from the hospital. I knew how much the girls loved their mum, they always had so much fun with her, and they would laugh non-stop. This would crush their little hearts.

Dad broke the news to the girls. They took the news as well as can be expected, dad on the other hand turned to what most Brits do-alcohol.

At first I was devastated for him and understood he was grieving, however, dad's drinking wasn't slowing down, it was getting worse. I was so scared and in my mind the girls had already lost a parent. Due to dad's grief, he potentially was going to put the innocent girls through this heartbreak all over again.

The tension grew in the house and I struggled being around him. Dad and I had never been great at communicating and, to be honest, my self-limiting belief of 'don't speak your truth' was holding back the words I wanted to say. I was there for the girls and to look after them, that was my role and to make sure I was doing my best for them. I started feeling trapped physically and emotional, in a dark place. I began shutting down from all communication with friends and family, as I would just snap at everyone due to feeling angry and let down by my dad. The biggest emotion I was dealing with was an overwhelming sense of responsibility for my sisters. I was trying my best to be there for them, however, my self-limiting belief; 'You're not good enough' was sitting shotgun. This then led me to become even more depressed, as I thought and was telling myself that I was letting the girls down and it felt like I wasn't supporting them properly. I started struggling with simple tasks, became forgetful and so overwhelmed.

I would never ask for help as thought it was a sign of weakness, however I was suffocating and felt so lonely. It's hard to think positively about yourself or anything for that matter when you're drowning in an ocean of negative thoughts.

One afternoon it all got a heated in the house, Dad and I had a blazing row and I let it all out and then guess what?... stormed out. #Historyrepeatingitself.

I went to stay with a friend for a few days to collect my thoughts. From that moment I decided it was best if I was out of the house when dad was home.

For the next few months that's how it remained, dad would come home from work, I would leave, or he would come home from the pub, the girls and me would be in bed. It was perfect; we became ships passing in the night. However, I was still stuck in darkness, as my identity had completely gone now and I couldn't communicate with anyone let alone with dad.

Spring had sprung and with that came a little fun! In previous years I had worked as a grid girl for the British Touring Car Championship and race season was about to get started. I absolutely loved it, the buzz I felt when at the track was incredible and the best part is I morphed into a happier, bouncier person. I had made amazing friendships with people in the paddock and I was grateful for that. It was my escape from reality.

Things were looking up and I started seeing a driver. From the outside I looked happy, spending time with friends, this guy and keeping busy. However, have you ever been so unhappy that when someone comes into your life and creates joy, you cling to that? You tell yourself you're happy and this guy is your soul mate and everything you have been looking for, however it's just a story.

Well, I did and I fell for the story HARD! I had known him for years and we shared lots in common, so it sounded like fairy tale. Driver rescues sad, lonely grid girl from her own shitty little life. What a headline!

Because he knew my situation and always praised me for stepping up to support my sisters, he made me feel worthy and understood. A feeling I hadn't felt before, resulting in me ignoring all the red flags that popped up during the relationship. Again, not setting any boundaries, I wanted to spend all my time with him, showered him with gifts and even started to imagine our future. Through the relationship we had some incredible times together, a short trip to Italy to watch Ferraris race, Karaoke night in his kitchen for my birthday, and he made every touring car weekend so special to watch, plus we spent the most amazing weekend at his sister's wedding. Sadly, I was bat shit crazy and thinking he was the ONE! Obviously, he wasn't on the same page, come Christmas the dreaded break up, on FaceTime can you believe?

(We have to thank Steve Jobs for the incredible technology these days - no longer do we have to deal with the breakup text now we have the breakup FaceTime! RIP Steve).

Sobbing my heart out as I hung up trying to understand what had just happened. I had let my guard down, told him I loved him, and then 20 days before Christmas, he bailed. This was the cherry on top of the ice cream; this was NOT my year and was the start of my self-destruct. I hated myself. Beating myself up daily, going over and over in my mind how it could have been different. Crying my eyes out in the car when Dua Lipa 'Don't start now' would come on the radio. (Which was every 10 minutes, thank you Kiss FM) I had no motivation for anything, didn't want to get out of bed, didn't want to eat, all I wanted was to be alone.

My dear old friend depression was back!

Confirming all my self-limiting beliefs; You're not good enough, you're unlovable, don't speak your truth and have nothing to show for myself. I began thinking terrible thoughts, going over in my mind how I could end my pathetic existence. I had a few different ideas, some more graphic than others but one thing was holding me back. I would think, I can do it today but then would panic; someone would need to collect my little sisters from school. The thought of the girls going through another death this year upset me more than my lonely, depressed life. I was trapped in a miserable, black, depressing hole and couldn't even kill myself as had no childcare #fucksake.

Not being able to talk to anyone about how I felt was increasing the depression, I couldn't talk to friends as they all agreed the breakup was for the best and I deserved better! Why does everyone say that when you're in a lot of pain? Clearly that's not what you want to hear at that point in time.

I felt devastated and lost. I had lost my best friend and the one person I felt happy around. I was grieving again but this time for my potential future.

Christmas was here and I couldn't bear the thought of pretending to be happy while opening a pair of socks from Primark. I had always despised Christmas, as in the past it's always been a painful time of year, rushing around between divorced parents houses, being told there isn't enough space for you at the dinner table now your little sisters have arrived. Just a lot of negativity and hurtful behaviour. I would definitely crack if I heard driving home for Christmas by Chris Rea, I decided I would do what I do best ... Run! Skip Xmas!

I booked a trip to Amsterdam with a travelling company. The company host trips around the world for back packers, so I knew there would be a few people also skipping Christmas. So excited to leave, I explained to mum that I had to get away for my own sanity and thankfully my mum was so understanding and luckily my sisters were with their aunt so I didn't have to worry about them.

December 23rd and I left for Amsterdam and instantly made friends with an Australian girl. We were both at the back of the bus chatting away and ended up sharing a room together. The tour guide, who was also Australian, was so sarcastic and hilarious, he had me in stitches all week long, exactly what I needed. I felt like I had known him for years. During the trip I experienced some wild activities like, clog making, sex shows, canal cruises and on Christmas Day we all sat down and enjoyed a Chinese buffet, my fav! The trip was exactly what I needed, a week of fun, laughter, and lots of alcohol with incredible people who were now new friends.

I returned home upbeat but still had no plan, however, I was not thinking terrible thoughts. I knew I had to seek help from a professional but didn't want anti-depressants as I felt that was masking the problems not dealing with them. My mum suggested a life coach; she had met a lady a few months before and shared her contact details with me. I researched into life coaching and found they focus on the future. Firstly, they see where you currently are and then help you to achieve your potential, this sounded perfect to me as I had no clue where I was going or what I was doing in the future.

# Part Two

In Part 2 of the Mindset Mission I will be sharing all the tools and techniques that have helped me rewire my unkind mind. There are 7 main techniques I couldn't live without and I hope you love them as much as I do.

Some of the tools, your ego mind might scream, "WTF are you doing?"

However, all I ask is you try all of them and please trust me and the process, granted not every tool will be for you, however, all I ask is please try.

I feel like my Nan, she would always say, "Try the vegetables, how do you know if you don't like them?"

Which is very true, you don't know if you don't try! The ego mind is very smart as it's there to protect us so doesn't like change however you are reading this book to change your mind set for the better so please override the ego mind and throw yourself into this part of the book.

I hope you enjoy and please reach out to me if you need any help or want to share your progress!

# Talking

After returning back from Dam I had decided that 2020 was the year to focus on me. I wanted to feel happier and healthier within myself but not go down the anti-depressants route. I know for some people this is the best option, however for me, I knew if I started I would struggle to come off them. A close friend explained to me that I might be masking the problem not facing it and straight away I knew I had to start talking about how I felt instead of numbing and avoiding. While in Amsterdam I had spoken to the people in the group, who started off as strangers and who were now friends, about how I felt and it really helped me. However, the stranger element was important to me, as I didn't feel comfortable talking to my friends or family. They obviously want the best for me but sometimes their opinions are reflected back or they tell you, "You're alright" and use the famous line, "Ah people have it worse"

I'm very aware people have it worse however I couldn't give a fuck right now I'm upset, I have been dumped, just let me be sad! Then I feel worse as now I'm a terrible person that, in this exact moment, is not super upset about starving children in Africa! Maybe you relate to this?

Talk therapy has become more popular now, which is incredible, whatever form you decide to use. For me talking about my situation with a coach really helped, as with life coaching, it focuses on the current reality and then encourages you to focus on the future. During the sessions I was able to talk about everything very openly, honestly and without judgement. It shifted my view on a lot of the shit that had got me to breaking point and really made me focus on the future.

Now I've got to a place where I can send love and gratitude to these experiences, for building a stronger Dani. For example, I am grateful for living at home and looking after my sisters, as it has built a strong loving relationship between them and me. Whereas before I saw this as a step back in my independence and felt a lot of pressure looking after the girls, which really nothing has changed, it all comes down to a positive switch in my mind.

Being able to become aware of the situation and the current reality (I don't like calling them problems; that's negative) it helps you to understand how you can change the situation, what your alternatives are, where you can place your energy to move forward and change your mindset. It made me realise and become aware that my life was worthwhile. I had so much to offer, so much love to share and, more importantly, focus and drive for the future.

So, let's use the CR tool and become aware of your current reality. Using the Heptagram example below, have a think of 7 key life areas and then score them 0-10 on satisfaction currently. I repeat currently!

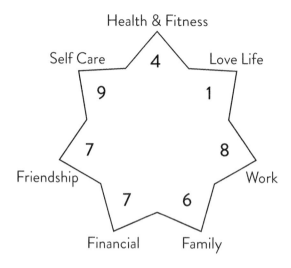

An example of CR Tool Heptagram

Once we become aware of current situations, feelings and emotions we can begin to work on them. Awareness is so important for growth so fill in your own Heptagram and see what comes up.

Like I said above, there is no judgement in coaching which allowed me to fully open up, become very emotional and still feel safe in sessions, which was very uplifting and powerful. Having someone to talk too really helped me to process and actually feel these emotions instead of bottling it all up and becoming resentful. I worked 121 with a coach for 6 months and, once that came to a natural end, I decided to join a group program with 9 others, everyone wanting to level up and achieve greatness. This group was incredible for me, having daily encouragement, surrounded by positive energy and support really made me blossom and start achieving my dreams.

MindWise states social connection is so important not just for our emotional wellbeing but our physical health as well. Feeling supported, listened to and not judged is very beneficial for the soul. I encourage you to speak to those around you if you feel comfortable they will hold a safe space for you without judgement or opinion. If not, reach out to me or another life coach or a group program as having cheerleaders in life, really keeps you motivated and positive. Connection and building relationships helps us as humans, feel happier and motivated. Psychiatrist Robert Waldinger is a director of a 75-year on-going study of what makes a happy life, and the research shows that good relationships is the key to happiness. I recommend watching the Ted Talk.

Of course, I still have bad days however, I know I have a great group of supportive people and I have also now learnt to sit with my emotions. I allow myself to cry, I have cried LOADS this year, on coaching calls, to myself but not once to sleep like 2019. I believe facing the feelings there and then has helped. It's actually reduced my bounce back rate. What I mean by a bounce back rate is how long it takes you to bounce back to happy and out of a negative mood. Please don't think you can change this in a day, a week or even a month. It takes a lot of practice and a few more tools I will discuss later in the book. One mentor helped me with dealing with my emotions and shared a model called FAN with me. FAN Stands for:

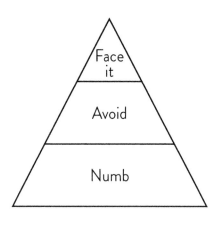

FAN model

Back in 2018 and 2019 I would avoid and numb my feelings daily, which resulted in me wanting to end my life. I would numb by drinking a lot, crave sex non-stop and eat shit foods. I would avoid my emotions and feelings by binge watching Netflix, hours and hours of scrolling on social media and online shopping. Never getting to the third tier of the model and facing the emotions, feelings and situations. It is important to face the situation because bottling it up only creates negative energy, which then attracts more negative energy.

The great T Harv Eker states:

*Your thoughts create your feelings.*
*Your feelings create your actions*
*Your actions create your results.*

My previous negative mindset was definitely creating more shit, for example: why I attracted people who didn't love me as my negative mind was telling me I'm unlovable. Not facing my emotions and feelings but avoiding them and numbing them created a very unhappy Dani who would snap at everyone, cry herself to sleep and became unmotivated about everything. Once I began to focus on my thoughts, it allowed me to have more control of my feelings and that became my goal, to work on my mindset and create more positivity in my mind.

**Golden Nuggets in this chapter:**

▶ CR Tool – Fill out your Current Reality Heptagram to become aware of your shitty situations.

▶ Talk to friends and family if you feel comfortable in doing so knowing you won't be judged, and they won't impose their opinions on you. If that's not the case reach out to me, I'm happy to talk to you or choose another life coach or a group program.

▶ Use the FAN model when you feel down in the dumps, notice if you are numbing, avoiding and please face it. It will be uncomfortable, but I promise it will be worth it and will overtime reduce your bounce back rate.

▶ Remember your energy or your vibe, whatever you want to call it, is so important. Become aware of your thoughts and try to stay positive – later in the book I share other tools to help this.

# How could you introduce this tool into your life?

# Meditation

Meditation is a fantastic tool to calm the unkind mind and start switching the mindset to a positive one. When I first got introduced to meditation I struggled, as I couldn't calm my thoughts and I would feel so distracted during it. Literally sitting with my eyes closed, not really listening to the lady on the app, thinking about food, or my ex or why my sisters were fighting right outside my bedroom door when they have the whole house? I hated sitting there as I thought I was wasting my time and energy, however, when we learn to drive a car you don't jump into the car and know how to control and drive straight away, it takes practice. You have to keep having lessons and showing up. Same with meditation, you don't just sit down close your eyes and automatically know how to control and calm your mind.

In the beginning I thought meditation was meant to stop all thoughts and you had to sit there for hours on end humming. This is the biggest myth; meditation is all about becoming aware of your thoughts and emotions NOT stopping them.

I started practising more but I still wasn't in a routine, so I didn't understand the thrill the yogis and monks talked about. Luckily, I then came across an interview held by Calum Best on Instagram. I was following him as who doesn't love some eye candy? Anyway, he had started a new series called Conscious Living, he was hosting interviews with lots of different coaches. They were all about mindfulness and wellbeing. One coach really aligned with me. Her energy was so warm and uplifting and during the meditation I felt so calm. Every week I would tune in and I began to experience some incredible insights during the meditations. I then came across another hunk with the bluest eyes ever on Instagram who delivered daily meditations and my creativity increased, this made my opinion on meditation change. I was really enjoying the Instagram lives and began falling in love with meditation.

Once I started practising daily I began feeling and seeing the benefits so much more, some benefits I have personally felt are:

- ▶ Improved self-awareness and self-image
- ▶ Reduced stress and anxiety
- ▶ Improved sleep pattern
- ▶ Increased attention span
- ▶ Improved creativity.

The first thing that I noticed was my sleep improving, especially as I was meditating around 7.30pm for around half hour. From 8-9pm I would try to keep my body relaxed by either, running a hot bath or reading, both very relaxing exercises which encourages sleep. Then come 9pm I would chill in bed journaling (which I will go into more detail later in the book) and planning for the next day. Come 9:30/10pm I was all dribs and snores. And I wonder why I'm single????

Secondly, my anxiety about the current global pandemic and lockdown, what other people thought of me and other life stresses began to minimise. I noticed I was standing up for myself if need be and not getting upset about it, I wasn't calling my mum to stress about tiny problems. Overall, I was becoming more pleasant to be around and more cheerful, which became very transparent in the household. I was connecting more with everyone including my dad, having deeper conversations at dinner, and enjoying them. It became clear, however still crazy to me, that if I focused on myself everything and everyone could benefit.

Thirdly my self-awareness and image improved. I didn't want that glass of wine at dinner and I respected myself enough to say no. I was looking deeper into my life, what I enjoyed and what I want to spend my time doing. Allowing myself to be the real Dani, not wearing make up every day and still feeling confident even for that Instagram selfie; instead embracing who I am, being natural and being proud. The summer of lockdown was such a powerful time for me to discover who I am as a person and meditation really started that. From such an uplifting experience with this tool, I have now qualified as a meditation coach and created a weekly stretch and meditation class, which has had incredible feedback from my clients, they have experienced benefits such as:

▶ Reduced blood pressure
▶ Improved memory
▶ Increased confidence
▶ Reduced judgement thoughts

The benefits my clients have experienced are incredible, meditation is helping them physically not just mentally and emotionally.

MindWorks have shared studies that prove a daily meditation practice improves blood circulation, lowers the heart rate and helps maintain a healthy heart. Studies also show cortisol production decreases in those who meditate daily. Cortisol is the hormone that is released when you are stressed. These are just a few studies out there proving meditation helps physically as well as mentally and emotionally, however please go do your own research on this very beneficial tool.

You may be asking yourself how do I meditate? I'll share how I meditate step by step and hopefully you can adopt this practice.

### Step 1 – The Environment
I have a meditation space in my house, my living room. Before, I would try and meditate on my bed, however that would just send me to sleep so now I have moved my practice downstairs, you need to be in a calm and quiet environment.

### Step 2 – Set the Mood:
I believe this is super important to calm the body and let yourself fully relax. I light candles and recently I bought a universe projector light so I switch that on really creating calmness around me.

### Step 3 – Creating Comfort:
You can lie down or sit up straight, just make sure you are comfortable. I make sure I have a blanket, as I often get cold during meditation.

## Step 4 – The Zone:

You can use apps or YouTube is also great. I have shared a lovely meditation with you below, and if you head over to my website you can download the meditation for free and listen to me deliver.

Whatever meditation you pick be fully open during the practice. If you are brand new I would recommend a shorter meditation 8-15 minutes and then, as you become more experienced, increase the time. Remember it takes practice!

# Welcome to this Love & Empowered Meditation

Tonight we are going to focus on our wonderful selves but first lets focus on our breath.

I would like you to get comfortable and close your eyes.

Breathe in and out naturally and just notice your breath. Is your breath shallow or deep?

*Inhale and exhale.*

Follow your breath into your body, where does it go down to – into your chest or your belly?

*Inhale and exhale.*

You haven't got to be anywhere, and you haven't got do anything right now. Give yourself permission to fully let go and be here in this moment. Relax.

You are allowing yourself time for self-care, you are here to quiet the mind and send yourself love.

So, what we are going to do is say some loving, powerful affirmations to ourselves, you may say them out loud if you wish or silently in your mind.

Repeat after me:

*I am strong*
*I am love*
*I am proud*
*I am enough*
*I am safe*
*I am worthy*
*I am brave*
*I am alive*
*I am connected to the universe*
*I am ready to succeed*
*I am always growing*
*I am healthy*
*I am gentle with myself*
*I am empowered*
*All that I seek is already within me*
*Everything happens for a reason*

*I can do anything I set my mind to. I'm empowered*

Know you have the ability to create whatever you wish in life. Your thoughts create your feelings and your feelings lead to actions, your actions create results.

Be kind and positive in your mind and be clear. A mentor once said to me, when you go to a restaurant do you ask for food or do you look at the menu and tell the waiter exactly what you want?

You can do anything you set your mind to, you're empowered, you're incredible, you're a creator.

Now bring your focus to your heart, you may place a hand over your heart if you wish to fully connect. Feel your heartbreak pumping all your blood around your amazing body and know you're alive! Now connecting to your heart and knowing you're a powerful being, what do you want? I'm the waiter asking, if you could create anything in your life, what would it be?

For a few minutes I want you to connect and visualise.

Amazing, Well done.

Now when you are ready. Bring your focus and your awareness back to this moment. Feel the sensations all over your body. And Slowly. Gently. I Invite you to open your eyes and just be still.

*Namaste.*

If I don't meditate daily my mind becomes foggy. Not taking that time to stop and check in and becoming aware of my emotions can really affect me. Becoming aware of your emotions actually neutralises them and allows you to refocus. If I don't make time to do this process it makes me ratty, irritable and resentful. I need that self- care to keep me positive.

Have you ever tried to pour wine out of an empty bottle before? No of course not! You need the wine to be able to enjoy the glass (or the bottle).

A lot of us, including old Dani, try to work on empty, whether that is low energy, lack of food, lack of sleep, however you don't perform at your best if you're not feeling your best. Selfcare is the same; you need to top up your battery daily like you would your Iphone. Meditation can do that! Charge your batteries, it's important.

From personally feeling some of the above benefits I now meditate a few times a day. I have a beautiful morning routine, which includes a 5-10 minute meditation that motivates me and sets me up nicely for the day. Like I said before I used to think you had to meditate for hours on end, however that is not the case at all, if you have a quiet, comfortable space you can do it for as little as a minute. You can do it anywhere, in bed, on a park bench or even at your desk at work. In fact, if I'm having a stressful day I try to remove myself for 5-10 minutes just to refocus and shift the mind. Luckily for me I now work from home but if I'm struggling with writing or nervous about coaching a new client, I stop, check in with myself, become aware with what's going on inside and refocus.

Breathing techniques are so incredibly powerful they can help change your mood, reduce your heart rate and allow you time to think about the situation. Like I said becoming aware is key as if you're not aware you can't change it or refocus.

## Golden Nuggets in this chapter:

▶ Meditation takes practice!
▶ It doesn't have to be for hours on end
▶ It has so many benefits, physical, mental and emotional.
▶ Meditation is for everyone, not just the Yogis & Monks.
▶ Don't fill your wine glass with an empty bottle, self-care is important.
▶ I host a weekly stretch and meditation class, which you are more than welcome to come and try, join us in calming your unkind mind.

# How could you introduce this tool into your life?

# Journaling

Journaling is such a powerful tool to help with stress and anxiety. Positive Psychology state there are many benefits to journaling such as:

▶ Mood Booster
▶ Reduces stress
▶ Increases working memory
▶ Releases pent up feelings and everyday stresses
▶ Increases self awareness

Unfortunately, journaling is often overlooked as a teenage girl ritual, writing their crush's name all over the page, however it's available for everyone with no limitations. You could write a few words on your Iphone or buy a beautiful journal that you really connect with. You can journal daily, weekly or whenever you feel you need too. I journal daily and would highly recommend it however everyone is different so do what works for you.

Journaling is a great way to become aware of your mindset and really helped me realise my thoughts, the process of getting the thoughts out of your head and on to paper really highlights what sort of state your mind is in. It's also a great reflection tool, looking back to a negative entry can really increase your mood and mindset knowing how far you have come. Here are a few journaling prompts I personally use.

# Comparison Journaling

Before, I would let everything build up in my head until I exploded, or worse, start making up stories in my head. One of the main negative thought patterns in my mind was comparison. Not with celebrities on Instagram but with people close to me. I would beat myself up; letting my ego mind get the better of me. Make myself feel like a complete piece of shit because I had moved home, taken a step back in my mind meanwhile my group of friends were buying houses and getting married. I made myself feel like the black sheep. I told myself they think I'm a loser and getting nowhere in life when in fact no one had EVER said such things.

When I found journaling I would write all these stories down and really get emotional while writing them to see whom I was comparing myself to, why I was comparing and what was making me think this way and how does this comparison make me feel? It was a great release getting the story out of my head and on to page; I like to believe once you have written the thought it is down on the page and your mind passes the responsibility to the journal. It clears my mind slightly. Many mentors say don't read your journal back, however I love to read it back as normally I think to myself, where have you got this bullshit from? It's a great reflection tool and, like I said, a great way to understand your current mind's state. I believe this tool could have really helped me during my relationship, as I was always telling myself he didn't want to be with me and found evidence to prove that to myself. If I had known about journaling then I could have got all my emotions out of my head and stopped badgering him and torturing myself in the process.

# Gratitude Journaling

Journaling daily about things, people and situations you are grateful for really helps me and keeps my mind positive. A mentor showed me this technique, to write 10 things I was grateful for. 5 in the morning and 5 at night reflecting back on the day.

Here is an example:

*11th April 2020*
*Morning*

*I am grateful for:*
- ▶ *Waking up this morning and feeling positive.*
- ▶ *Having a peaceful night's sleep.*
- ▶ *The sun shining today.*
- ▶ *Everyone being home during lockdown, so I know we are all-safe.*
- ▶ *For my productive day ahead.*

I love to write as if it has already happened; it helps to manifest the act itself and feels me with joy. Then in the evening it's a reflection of the day.

*Evening*

*I am grateful for:*
- ▶ *The garden, I sat out there all-day making memories with the girls.*
- ▶ *My credit card – It has allowed me to purchase an apple watch.*

- ▶ *My friends all over the world, connected with Simon Mitchell (incredible friend and coach).*
- ▶ *My bath – love reading while having a soak.*
- ▶ *My new pjs that I'm currently snuggled in as I write this entry.*
- ▶ *My incredibly funny and supportive brother, so lucky to have him.*

They could be small or big but get into a routine of documenting and it really makes you appreciate and see there are always positives. Oprah Winfrey says it perfectly:

*"The more you praise and celebrate your life,
the more there is in life to celebrate".*

So powerful and so true, so start a daily gratitude list to become aware and appreciate everything you have now. I'll go into more detail about gratitude later in the book.

## Proud Lists

Another great journaling technique I love is to create proud lists. A list of everything you have achieved, big or small, that makes you feel proud, which moving back home to help my dad with my sisters was right up there. In fact, my ego mind and the alcohol intake were making my mind fuzzy and playing games with me, however it was so great having it documented so I could look at it with fresh eyes. Other examples on the proud list would be, creating book club, meditating daily, helping Thames21 charity and, of course, a huge one signing my publishing deal.

I normally write a proud list monthly to reflect, be appreciative and grateful however, a mentor recently suggested I start writing them daily as I really struggle with celebrating my success. And knowing the quote from Oprah mentioned above I need to work on this ASAP. I then thought of the quote by Peter Sheppard Skaerved:

> *"Find happiness, by enjoying the journey, not by awaiting the destination".*

This really hit home for me and is so true. We all need to stop telling ourselves we will be happy when... we lose 2 stone or once I have a boyfriend and start being grateful and proud of who we are and what we have NOW!

The Gratitude journaling and proud lists will help with this.

I have now adopted the proud list daily, here is an example for you:

*4th December 2020*

- ▶ *I showed up for a Zoom session today and created action points straight after.*
- ▶ *Helped my sister with her homework.*
- ▶ *Researched into a new business venture involving meditation.*
- ▶ *Held a beautiful space for a private meditation client.*
- ▶ *Ticked off a few more action points on my 6-week goal.*

# Brain Dump

Another mentor introduced me to the 'Brain Dump' Exercise This is grabbing your pen the second you open your eyes and jotting down everything that comes to mind. I like to put a timer on my watch for 5 minutes and literally, every thought that comes to mind I write down.

Could be: *I need a pee or is my sister up for school?*

It's a great way to again become aware of the thoughts there and then, after the 5 minute sprint you can analyse and maybe see what you would like to focus on that day, or if there is anything urgent you need to do i.e.) pee or send your lovely nan a happy birthday text. Yes my Nan is 89 and texts!

# Dream Journaling

Sometimes if I have vivid dreams, I like to write them down just so I can have a reflective giggle or try to see what my subconscious mind is telling me. As Sigmund Freud famously described dreams as a window into the subconscious. I find this all very fascinating; I know it's not for everyone and can sound a bit WOO WOO but even if it gives you a little giggle with friends and family, it's a positive to me. Once I had a very positive and passionate dream about Max Verstappen and I. Let's just say Max, if you're reading this, slide into my DMs!! Obviously, my subconscious mind wants Max and I to live happily ever after.

All jokes aside, I love journaling everything in my life, the good, the bad and the ugly (Great movie) It allows me to release the burdens, appreciate the wins and, the best part, be able to reflect back and see my growth, however, like I said earlier in this chapter, you can write about future events which encourages you and the manifestation of the thing, person, event and or act.

For example, every day I write in my journal:

*I am a Best Selling Published Author.*

Inspiring me to keep working hard delivering this book, which leads me on to the final journal exercise.

## A Day in a life.

This last exercise I got introduced to and really enjoy, which I now encourage all my clients to do, is to write a day in a life of your future self-including every detail. Here are some prompt questions you can answer to create your own vision.

*What time do you wake up?*
*Who do you spend the day with? Husband? Kids? Pets? Best friend?*
*What do you do for work?*
*Where do you live?*
*Do you have hobbies?*
*What are you wearing?*

Creating this crystal-clear vision of how you want your life to pan out and reading it daily is a great manifesting tool. Remember T Harv Eker:

> *Your thoughts create your feelings.*
> *Your feelings create your actions*
> *Your actions create your results.*

So, reading your 'Day in a life' will create positive feelings, which will encourage you to act towards your day in a life, creating incredible results!!

I have created my own Day in a life in 2 years' time. I'll share it for inspiration.

*My alarm goes off, its 6:30am. I roll over and grab my journal for my morning 'Brain Dump' exercise, clearing my head before I start the day. Springing out of bed as I'm used to my morning routine by now. I go into the bathroom to brush my teeth and wash my face. Heading down my beautiful, open planned staircase into my white, marbled kitchen to put the kettle on, a strong builder's cup of tea is needed. Heading into my newly decorated office, I get cosy in the turquoise velvet love seat to read the monthly book club book for half hour, while enjoying my English tea. Once my watch timer alerts me I have completed 30 minutes, I get even more comfortable, grab a blanket and close my eyes to begin my morning energising mediation.*

*10-15 minutes later, feeling abundant and full of energy I turn on my Bose ceiling speakers and connect to my raise the vibe Spotify playlist, which now has 5.4 million followers. I hit shuffle and #that Power by Will.i.am & Justin Bieber comes on, I dance around my office, waving in scents sticks and singing at the top of my lungs. Luckily, my fiancé has left for the track already; he is a racing driver. I open the shutters on the bay window to look out on to the beach. I am grateful for my stunning view and privacy while dancing around like a tit, raising my vibration and getting myself ready to smash the day. Once danced like no one was watching, I sit at my clean and organised desk to plan the day, prioritizing the most important tasks.*

*Once organised, I head back upstairs and get showered and dressed. All glam, my day starts at 9am with a team meeting, to discuss the on-going events this week, for example:*

▶ *How many meditation classes are being held on what days and at what times, which instructor will be hosting?*

▶ *As we just reached 1 million book sales (YAY – Thank you). Do I have any book signings events this week? If so where and when?*

▶ *Am I needed at the racetrack at the weekend, to support the F1 race team I work with?*

*After an important and very informative meeting, I have a 121 coaching client, where I hold the space and support the client to reach their potential. Lunchtime, I treat myself and any team members I have at the house that day, to my favourite Italian restaurant down by the beach front, where we share delicious food. I'm a huge fan of the prawn linguine and we share a mojito mocktail before heading back home to continue the day.*

*The afternoon is more relaxed than the morning, as I believe the best way to work is to focus your undivided attention for short periods of time to achieve the greatest, rather than half-hearted long days. I will check on my social media and reply back to my readers' questions, maybe host an Instagram live or a meditation class to really engage with everyone.*

*Once 4pm rolls around, that's my workday done and now to focus on my gorgeous bulldog Kika and my fitness routine. Out for a beach run followed by a personal training session in the garage. I'm very lucky to have a fabulous trainer who comes to me 5 times a week. Straight in a hot bubble bath, where I take that important self-care time and reflect on the productive day.*

*Dinnertime; my loving fiancé or me will cook and share the yummy meal together outside on our decking overlooking the ocean, sharing our news from the day and a cuddle under the stars feeling so loved and grateful.*

*I'm off up to bed around 10pm as I know sleep is a huge factor to keeping healthy plus to keep to my busy routine. Before snoring the night away I first meditate again to calm the mind and relax the body ready for a perfect night's sleep.*

# Goodnight World xoxo

For those who have never journaled before I would suggest starting with the 'A Day in a life' so you can get excited for the future and create a positive experience with your first journaling experience. I would then encourage you to start the 'Brain Bump' exercise daily to become aware what your mind is saying when you first wake up. You can reflect weekly or monthly but please book in the time to look back as it's so important to become aware of the growth within you.

The Gratitude and Proud lists again, I would encourage you to do it daily to increase your mindset on everything you already have and what you have achieved. My mindset has improved massively since doing these exercises daily.

Comparison journaling is my favourite form of journaling as it calls you out on your own bullshit! It's a great tool to use when you are having a bad day, so I wouldn't recommend doing daily but know you have this tool in your locker to really rant, face the problem/ story and release it, resulting in calming your mind and mood. Remember it's then the journal who has the responsibility not your mind.

**Golden Nuggets in this chapter:**

► Journaling is for everyone not just teenage girls who are in love.
► It's proven to help with stress to keep a calm, clear mind.
► There are lots of difference techniques on how to journal.
► Please remember, keep your journal private, however, if you would like to share your Day in a life please contact me.

# How could you introduce this tool into your life?

# Reading

Before starting my self-development journey, I hadn't picked up a book since secondary school and even then I would take the book home and plead with my mum to read it chapter by chapter, telling me what happened so I wouldn't fail English class. Reading always bored me but in fact I was reading the wrong books. James Patterson said, "There's no such thing as a kid who hates reading. There are kids who love reading and kids who are reading the wrong books".

I couldn't agree more, once you find what you love to read you will enjoy reading.

In January 2020 I set myself a challenge to read a book a month to broaden my knowledge and increase my self-care. As you know there is nothing more satisfying then climbing into a hot bath and reading a book. I decided to only read positive material and mainly self-development books, as I definitely needed help with life and my mindset. The first book I read was a fiction book and told a story of a girl who become lost in life, I could totally relate so the book became glued to my hand. Every month my love for reading grew as I was learning lots of new techniques to create a positive mindset.

Healthline states reading helps with keeping the mind engaged, reduces stress, alleviates depression symptoms, which I can confirm reading most definitely helped me with reducing my stress levels, keeping my mind engaged which all helped with my state of mind and happiness.

Lockdown in UK had just come in to play, resulting in furlough. I had all this time on my hands, which I saw as a great opportunity to read more. I started reading a book called 'Don't dull my sparkle' by Doreen Virtue – OMG! I literally couldn't put the book down, finishing within a couple of days. It went into detail about how past trauma in life affects the brain and your mindset. I could relate to every single word in the book and felt like the author was talking directly to me. Have you ever felt like this when reading?

All my life I have said, "Oh I should write a book" with all the dramatic things that have happened and from increasing my reading I decided to start writing my story, sharing my voice and my journey. No idea did I believe we would be here today, with you holding this book in your hands!!

After reading 'Don't Dull my Sparkle', I reached out on my social media sharing what an incredible book it was and that reading was helping me through lockdown. Helping my anxiety, keeping me entertained and, as a bonus, I was learning as well. I asked on my Instagram if anyone wanted to join me, creating an online book club. I was completely blown away by the response. In May that was when The Positive Page Club was born and has grown from strength to strength every month since.

From reading such positive, supportive books it has made me understand the importance of feeding your mind positivity, but it's also allowed me to create and build a positive platform for others to join as well, our own inclusive, safe community, which is incredible. We have had authors come on and speak with us; we set each other challenges and hold space for each other.

It's a magic community and I always suggest to the book clubbers my Reading Kit that includes the vital tools for reading and fully engaging with the words on the page: #Dothebook

- ▶ A cup of tea (of course!)
- ▶ A candle to set the mood.
- ▶ A highlighter to emphasize any phrases or key points that resonates with you which helps with memory.
- ▶ Post- it tabs to stick at the top of the page making it easier to return to later if you want or need.
- ▶ A pretty bookmark so you don't have to ruin the edge of the book and can remember where you left off.

If you are stuck with what book to start with here is my recommended reading list:

- ▶ *Don't Dull My Sparkle* – Doreen Virtue
- ▶ *Happy* – Ferne Cotton
- ▶ *How To Be Perfectly Imperfect* – Candi Williams
- ▶ *One Thing* – Gary Keller & Jay Papasan
- ▶ *The Good Girl's Guide To Being A Dick* – Alexandra Reinwarth
- ▶ *The Life Magic Of Not Giving A F\*\*K* – Sarah Knight

- *The Miracle Morning* – Hal Elrod
- *Wake The F\*\*K Up* – Brett Moron

Please feel free to connect with us and join our monthly reading group, the more the merrier.

> **Golden Nuggets in this chapter:**
>
> - Decide today to pick up a book
> - Set yourself a goal to read a book a month
> - Buy a Reading Kit to make sure you're reading right!
> - If you need more support and accountability join us @thepositivepageclub_

# How could you introduce this tool into your life?

# Gratitude

Throughout my self-development journey gratitude has been huge. Every mentor I have had shared that being grateful for what you have will improve your happiness and mindset, plus you become more present in the moment. Robert Holden says it perfectly:

> *"The real gift of gratitude is that the more grateful you are, the more present you are."*

Being present in the moment has really helped me with my mood and state of mind. Before I was always in my head, listening to the ego mind and the stories non-stop and getting myself upset, angry or very anxious. Not being in the moment, not being grateful for my surroundings or the people in my life. Once I started shifting that through journaling and meditation, my mindset and mood changed, and I became more grateful and present.

'Forbes.com share being grateful' can have incredible benefits on your quality of life, they go on to share, Gratitude reduces a multitude of toxic emotions, ranging from envy and resentment to frustration and regret. Robert A. Emmons, Ph.D., a leading gratitude researcher, has conducted multiple studies on the link between gratitude and well-being. His research confirms that gratitude effectively increases happiness and reduces depression. I have experienced this first-hand my physical situation hasn't changed, however, through gratitude, I am so much happier and driven now.

We all hear and see the word gratitude nowadays which is fantastic, however, I believe it's an overlooked tool that we can adopt very easily into our day to day lives. Gratitude to me is being aware of your life, the people in it and highlighting all the positives, showing thanks and understanding, there is always a positive in any situation. I am now at the point where I am grateful for the past terrible experiences that have happened, as I know I have grown into a better, stronger woman because of them.

Here are a few things I'm grateful for everyday:

*I am so grateful for my relationship with my little sisters as, before I hardly saw them, and how my relationship with my dad has improved massively. We are still a work in progress, but we now enjoy each other's company and I know he does love and appreciate me.*

*I am so grateful for the breakup as now I know what sort of lover I am and what I need in a man moving forward, which I am being brave again and letting my wall down, opening my heart ready for Mr Right.*

*I am grateful for this self-development journey I will continuously be on as it has really shown me the things that were holding me back, my self-limiting beliefs I created in my head, and has allowed me to jump out my comfort zone and create incredible things, including this book.*

*I am grateful for everyone in my life, even the people who trigger me as they are teaching me lessons, I just have to breathe and workout what that lesson is.*

*I am grateful for all the people that have supported me along the way and helped me to grow.*

*I am grateful for myself as I now ask for help when it's needed instead of thinking it's a weakness.*

*I am grateful for all the abundance in my life and bank account, without money I couldn't experience and treat the people I love so I am very grateful for money and the positive energy it brings.*

*Most importantly I am grateful for my brother and mum, who have always been there for me no matter what. I am so fortunate!*

*I AM GRATEFUL!!*

I invite you to start today noticing the incredible things, people, moments in your life and write them down. Head back to the journaling chapter for a reminder.

I'm not sure who said this quote however it is so true.

> *"Everyday may not be good,*
> *but there is something good in every day".*

So start noticing and get out of your head, the pity party is OVER!
Be grateful, be happy, be proud and love everyone who comes into
your life, as they are all a blessing and teaching you something!

**Golden Nuggets in this chapter:**
- ▶ Grab your journal and start noticing the good things in your life
- ▶ Create a daily habit of noticing the good
- ▶ Awareness is key!

# How could you introduce this tool into your life?

# Cluttered Mind

Back in 2019 one thing that would cause me serious stress was feeling like I had nothing to work towards, no identity, no purpose, nothing to get out of bed for, however, now that's transformed into having a clear vision with the help of talking, meditating and questioning myself in my journal. If I'm not organised though I can feel overwhelmed and like I have no time to achieve, then self-doubt and the self-limiting beliefs make an appearance. I can't do this; who do I think I am? I'm not good enough.

I realised I must be super organised and planning helps with my stress levels and being overwhelmed, which results in a happier mindset and happier Dani.

Here are a few techniques I have used over the past year to keep my focus clear, positive and reduce my stress.

## Vision Boards

Many leaders and mentors encourage you to create vision boards and, at first I did think, how are a few photos going to help me? Sitting down for an hour or so and really thinking what you want in life, writing them down or drawing them out really creates a positive movement within your mindset and body, plus it's a great activity to do with your kids. I have done this a few times with my sisters, had a creative afternoon sharing our visions and goals. Placing your vision board somewhere you see every day, keeps reminding you and your subconscious mind what you are aiming for and keeps the drive alive. I have placed my vision board above my desk so every day, when working, if I look straight ahead I have my goals there. I drew my board out and coloured everything in so it stands out, but it is also personal plus creative. The great Patty Dobrowolski has an incredible Ted Talk all about drawing your vision boards, I highly recommend watching. Others like to cut pictures out of a magazine or create a board on Pinterest and print it out, whatever works for you. The vision board is key to keeping you motivated to work hard on your dreams, goals and desires.

HuffPost states "Visualization is one of the most powerful mind exercises you can do" which correlates with my favourite quote I have mentioned many times throughout this book.

*Our thoughts create feelings,*
*Our feelings create actions,*
*and our actions create results.*

T Harv Eker

What we see and think about is so important so focus on your dreams and think about them daily.

# Action Points

Action points are what create our goals, dreams into reality. If you have a dream and do nothing, guess what? Nothing will change so this step to uncluttering your mind is so important.

I like to break down my goals into months at a time and break it down further into week by week. This helps me to understand what I need to do and when. I write everything down on a whiteboard in my office, so I see it daily and it's clear. Before, I tried writing it down in my journal, however I would forget to check it and didn't have the daily reminder, resulting in not a whole lot.

Jim Rohn states:

> *"Goal setting is powerful because it provides focus. It shapes our dreams. It gives us the ability to hone in on the exact actions we need to perform, to achieve everything we desire in life."*

This is exactly why the action point plan is key to achieving your dreams. No plan, no dreams achieved.

I use my vision board to create the important factors to focus on to achieve the desired goal for example. On my vision board I have this book hitting number 1 on the Amazon book list.

Then on my action points I have:

*Week 1 - Finish the Cluttered Mind chapter and send to my publisher. If I don't finish the chapter then the book won't be complete. I can't achieve my goal of smashing the Amazon book list.*

*Week 2 - Edit the chapter once getting the feedback from my publisher.*

*Week 3 – Describe to the designer my vision for the book cover.*

*Week 4 – Relax and sit tight waiting for the designer's work.*

As you can see, every week I am one step closer to achieving my dream and that's what I would love you to create. A simple but effective check list of action points to achieve your wildest dreams.

Side Note: Huge Thank you for purchasing my book as you have helped me create my wildest dreams.

## Accountability calendar

My favourite tool!

I created this calendar to see if I was keeping up with my daily mindset routine aka DMR which has a direct effect on my productivity.

After reading an incredible book called; The Miracle Morning I created a similar Daily Mindset Routine (DMR) which, consists of:

*Journaling - J*
*Reading - R*
*Affirmations - A*
*Working out - WO*
*Meditating – M*

On the calendar, if the activity was completed that day, I mark using the Key above to show that. Weekly, I look back to see if any activities were missed, and if so, did it affect my productivity levels and or my mindset. At the end of the month, I look over again to see where I could improve, as I like to believe every day I can improve and get better.

For Example: November 2020 I only managed to work out 13 times which had a huge impact on my positive mind, so December came, and it was my mission to increase that, which I achieved.

Zen Shin shared:

> *"A flower does not think of competing to the flower next to it, it just blooms".*

This quote really hit home and made me think. As a society we all compare ourselves to each other, however, I am trying to change my mindset to only compare myself to my past self, as that's all that matters. If I have improved then I'm growing and blossoming into a beautiful flower.

## Golden Nuggets in this chapter:

- ▶ Action is Key!
- ▶ Create a vision board
- ▶ Create action points from the vision board
- ▶ Use the accountability calendar for your DMR
- ▶ Don't compare to anyone but you.

# How could you introduce this tool into your life?

# Mood Booster

## Dancing - #raiseyourvibe

When I first got introduced to dancing to change my mindset and energy, I generally thought WTF! However, it works so don't knock it until you try it. The other morning, I woke up in a mood, yes it was that time of the month but also I had woken up later than I had wanted which led to me half assing my morning routine. Instead of getting up straight when the alarm went off, brushing my teeth, drinking a glass of water then heading downstairs to meditate for 5-10 minutes, I stopped my alarm, slouched in my bed and started to meditate which caused me to fall back asleep. Waking up later than I had wanted, now not having enough time to meditate, or read, I was frustrated and could feel my energy was low. I had a coaching call first thing and I pride myself on showing up 100% for the client so I had to change my mood/ energy and mindset. On goes the Raise the Vibe playlist on Spotify (feel free to follow my playlist).

There I was dancing my heart out 10 minutes before my coaching client at 9:15am, music blasting out of my speaker and dancing my socks off. When we dance, our bodies release endorphins, aka the happy hormone, and this hormone makes us feel happier and can reduce stress. So, I challenge you to check out my Raise the Vibe playlist and dance out the stress, tagging me in a video, I'm holding you accountable.

# Fitness

As you all know I used to be a personal trainer and gym manager, so fitness has always played a part in my life. In 2019 I struggled with my motivation and time to get to the gym, which had a direct effect on my mood. When lockdown first hit my amazing brother decided to turn one of the garden sheds into a gym. I literally had no excuses not to train anymore however was still struggling. I reconnected with a personal trainer friend and we started competing together via Apple watch, having that competition daily really encouraged me to workout. A few weeks later after being defeated by him, I decided to join an online PT program for accountability and structure to my workouts. This really helped me get my daily mojo back for working out. Like dancing it also allowed me to release endorphins creating a healthier, happier Dani.

Giving yourself that self-care by working out helps in so many ways not just physically; you mentally start feeling more confident and your self-love increases. If you struggle with fitness and nutrition I highly recommend getting a coach to help you, even if it's only for the first initial couple of weeks.

Once lockdown was lifted I decided to start Thai boxing, I had done it previously as a kid and loved it. I wanted a new challenge to get my teeth into. I was so nervous at first, however, after the first couple of sessions I felt like superwoman. My coach is so empowering and encouraging he really makes me feel like I'm the strongest client he has ever had. For me it's great fitness as on a normal session I burn up to 500 calories but also I'm learning a new skill and self-defence. I highly recommend trying a new sport and getting an accountability buddy as then you're more likely to show up if you have someone else relying on you too.

# Cooking

When I first moved back into the family home, dad would cook most of the time but I decided I wanted to cook more so bought a few recipe books and started getting creative. Blasting the tunes while preparing food would really boost my mood and then knowing I had created the meal for the evening would fill me with gratitude.

My little sister is in year 9 at school and has cooking as one of her subjects, during lockdown she had to cook various meals, cakes etc and send photos to her teacher as proof. My sister and I would create whatever was needed for her subject, we really enjoyed this time together, and bonding over cake was definitely a highlight of lockdown for me. Now we regularly cook together, as we both enjoy it plus my little sister is learning new dishes. I personally believe if you cook with love and fun you enjoy the meal so much more. Cooking has now become an act of self-love I show others and myself. I highly recommend buying a decent recipe book and getting creative with your food, after all its our fuel and the better tasting and healthier it is the more enjoyment and energy we have.

# Hot baths

A super bubbly hot bath is one of favourite mood boosters. There is nothing better after a hard stressful day than slowly edging yourself into the roasting water, with a candle lit and soothing music playing in the background. This is another act of self-love, taking that time to be by yourself, pampering with Epsom salts and maybe reading your book or watching a Ted Talk during. Please try getting out of the bath still stressed and angry, it won't happen! #PureBliss

# Getting dressed

This may seem like a silly mood booster however, it wasn't until a personal stylist mentioned it to me, that I had even thought about it. During lockdown myself and a lot of the world had adopted the loungewear look. There's no harm in the loungewear look however, I had taken it a step to far, only washing my hair once a week and living in my PJs most days. It wasn't until the personal stylist said to me, when you make an effort with your appearance, do you feel better? With no hesitation I answered 'Of course'

She then went on to ask why I was not making an effort daily to make myself feel better? I was stumped. I had been doing everything for my mindset i.e.) meditation, journaling etc. however not getting up and dressing was negatively influencing my mind and mood. From the very next morning I got up an extra half hour earlier, did my morning routine, and then washed my hair, put my make up on and chose a nice outfit from my wardrobe. Instantly I felt ready and confident for the day. So, it may seem silly but always dress to impress as it increases your mood, your confidence and happiness!

# Reiki

Reiki is an energy healing practice, which originates from Japan. Reiki mainly focuses on stress reduction, relaxation and healing. The technique looks at all aspects of the client, including emotions, the mind and body. It's an incredible deep meditation that sooths and clears all low vibrating energies from the body.

My first ever experience honestly left me feeling like I was on cloud 9 for days after. Reiki has opened my eyes to the importance of energy and flow within the body. It has increased my energy levels and has allowed my mind to settle through the meditation during the practice. It's an amazing feeling during and after, definitely boosts my mood and I highly recommend you trying it.

In closing this Chapter I want to state that when emotions arise please do not ignore the feelings and go back to the fan model in the talking chapter. Please do not numb and/or avoid the emotions. Face it, and once you feel it's all released try one or a few of the above mood boosters. Also, if you have any other ways of boosting your mood I would love to hear them so please reach out on social media and share with me, thank you and I hope this helps.

# How could you introduce this tool into your life?

# Me Now

Firstly, thank you so much for completing the book, I really hoped you enjoyed it and the content as much as I enjoyed writing the book. The process was challenging but also such a learning process, plus super fun! I still can't believe I have published a book! I strongly believe everyone has a book inside them, everyone has a story that needs to be heard. Growing up, whenever something dramatic would happen, as a joke I always said, "OMG, I should write a book" and it took a global pandemic to give me that time to sit down and write, so as weird as this sounds, I'm grateful for this crazy world we live in as now hopefully I'm helping you switch your mindset to become more positive, with a focus and drive for life.

I hope you took some golden nuggets away with you and have already started implementing them into your DMR. Please reach out and share your success and troubles along the way with me on social. I am so grateful for all of you and would love to hear about your experiences, so please don't hesitate.

The past year was an incredible time for me, I learnt so much about myself. I learnt my core values and what means the most to me. I worked out what my passion is and found my fight again. Fierce Dani is back baby!!

Today, I sit in my office with my beautiful bulldog snoring behind me, writing to you as a changed woman. I'm bouncier, always smiling and dancing around. Don't think I don't have bad days; however, my bounce back rate has increased massively and I'm not scared to feel my feelings anymore. I'm always looking at the glass half full not half empty like I used too. I know my values and have set boundaries that only complement my life. I am grateful for my past, as it's created the strong, driven woman who sits here now.

I'm still living at home and looking after my sisters; however, I have my purpose in place and now I have a great balance of big sister duties and me time. Plus, dad and I have a stronger relationship; he understands I need my time and a career for myself. I am so grateful that our relationship has grown, I have my dad back which floods me with such warmth. Over the past year we have shared some incredible moments together and we communicate a lot better.

My sisters and I share a beautiful, loving relationship filled with laughter. They are both such loving, caring girls. They are so strong and smart, sometimes they can be divas but all the best people are. I am so proud of the girls and I'm so thankful I have such an incredible relationship with them now.

My brother has been my absolute rock; he makes me die of laughter daily, which positively impacts my mindset. He also inspires me to keep working hard; he is younger than me and has such an incredible hunger for success. My mum has always been my biggest cheerleader and has supported me always, I'm so grateful December 2019 she understood how important it was for me to flee and find myself in Amsterdam as if that trip hadn't of happen who knows where I would be right now.

This past year has shown me just how strong I am and when I truly want something I will work my bollocks off to get it. I write to you proudly, sharing I am a published bestselling author and a mindset and meditation coach who truly loves what she does. I get such a buzz seeing my clients silencing their unkind minds and smashing their potential. Getting calls of excitement honestly fills me with so much love and I'm proud I didn't listen to my unkind mind when it was telling me to give up.

I have also realised that during my entire life I have had such supportive, loving people around me and those that weren't supporting me mentally and/or physically, I have taken a step back from, as I needed time for me and needed to know I was being held by the correct people. It's funny as when you're younger, being popular is probably the most important thing, then as you get older, having fewer friends who truly love you for you and who lift you up, is the most important. This became so clear during my mindset mission.

Now on to the elephant in the room, yes, I'm still single, however this year I'm putting even more focus on myself and working on my unkind mind around my love life, which still holds on to the self-limiting belief; I am unlovable. I continuously work with a coach to explore my self-limiting beliefs and any other subject that comes up which I need help with. I will always invest in myself and create the support network I need to succeed in love, business and my mindset so, that being said, I'm holding myself accountable with you and sharing my big, bold intention for my next chapter:

*I am willing to open my heart back up and welcome a kind, supportive, affectionate man who will complement my life and me.*

I must say not much physically has changed in my life; however, my mindset has, and now my days are filled with purpose, gratitude and love. I wake up in the morning excited for the day ahead and know my DMR will set me up ready to smash whatever intention I have in place.

It's been a mad journey, but I wouldn't be where I am today without all the ups and downs. I have learnt we are exactly where we should be in life and trust the progress. I couldn't have dreamt my life would be what it is now back in December 2019 so thank you to everyone who has supported me and kept me accountable along the way. So grateful and happy!

My Mindset Mission is continuously on going and the next chapter has only just begun!

Love you all

Dani x

# Thank You!

Luke Whelan

Thank you for always making me feel like a superhero during every session. You made me realise I am unstoppable!

Thank you for being there for me through the thick of it and trusting me, volunteering to be my first ever coaching client. Love you forever.

Sarah Dennis

Thank you ladies, for all the support and encouragement. Always pushing me out of my comfort zone. Love you both dearly!

Jill Ritchie & Lynette Gray

Sean Murray

Sean, honestly I cant thank you enough for everything you have done for me. I am so grateful to you and That Guy's House. I cant believe we have a book out together!! Thank you for all the support over the past year and here's to book #2. EEKKK!

Thank you for all you do at Bodhi, you truly are a beautiful soul and I'm so grateful to now have you as a friend.

Georgia Langridge

Thank you for teaching me the art of meditation and calming down my Unkind Mind. Coconut on me when we see each other next!

Brett Moran

other thank you's:
Grace Harrison, Paul Simpson,
Megan McGrory, Emily Dann,
Becky Mulvanny, Joe Murphy
the Higham School Mums

Thank you for introducing me to Reiki and opening my mind to the power of energy.

Hailey Thomson

My family!!!

Luke – Thank you so much for always being there for me and making me laugh. I can always count on you and i'm so lucky to have you in my life.

India – Thank you for being the strongest, kindest young girl I know. I am so proud of you and your mum would be so proud too.

Dolly – Thank you for keeping me on my toes, being the little diva you are! Please don't ever change!

LOVE YOU ALL SO MUCH!

# Additional reading

Mindwise
https://www.mindwise.org/blog/uncategorized/the-impor-tance-of-social-connection/#:~:text=Help%20you%20olive%20longer%3A%20Research,50%25%20increased%20likeli-hood%20of%20survival.

Robert Waldinger, Ted Talk
https://www.youtube.com/watch?v=8KkKuTCFvzI

MindWorks
https://mindworks.org/blog/physical-mental-benefits-of-medi-tation/

Health line
https://www.healthline.com/health/benefits-of-reading-books

HuffPost.com
https://www.huffpost.com/entry/the-scientific-rea-son-why_b_6392274?guccounter=1&guce_referrer=aHR0cHM-6Ly93d3cuZ29vZ2xlLmNvbS88&guce_referrer_sig=AQA-AACteJ_QBz8MdQwZ4Yb3vNXFEqyZlyo2e6BvPlP3DCQy-jewop1u4s4S39sO47MF1aZieFh1rCkwsMPAC1ZQ2VEbhxgt-TdgzSt3o25PIooV3gyeY7rjuriALxWwNPCEMnegg7DPC8xG-BmRo7zjFeKxHvyP_ZblEsFlIemgoTdULRIn

Forbes.com

https://www.forbes.com/sites/amymorin/2014/11/23/7-scientif-ically-proven-benefits-of-gratitude-that-will-motivate-you-to-give-thanks-year-round/?sh=7a5c2a8a183c